Come in Here, CROCS!

Matt Reher · April Ferry

I am a crocodile.

2

This is one of my eggs.

3

What is in my eggs?

There are crocodile babies
in my eggs.

I have lots of eggs.

Where will my eggs go?

My eggs go in my nest.

Monitor Lizard

Lizards want to eat my eggs.

GRRRRRRR!!!

This is why I am here.

What is that?

It is my babies!

They want to come out
of the eggs.

13

This is a tooth.

And this is a tooth.

My babies have this tooth
to get out.

They swim with me.

They get up on my back.

Fish Eagle

Here comes an eagle.

He wants to get my babies.

What can I do?

Come in here, babies!

I am big.

I have big teeth.

He can't get my babies.

My babies live.

Fish eagles live near rivers and lakes in Africa. They catch their food with their strong feet and talons. They mostly eat fish, but they will also hunt for small monkeys, frogs, and crocodile babies.

crocodile's predators?

Nile monitor lizards are the largest lizards in Africa. They can grow to be 7 feet long. They are great hunters. These lizards eat fish, frogs, snakes, and birds. They can open their mouths wide to swallow large crocodile eggs.

Crocodile Anatomy

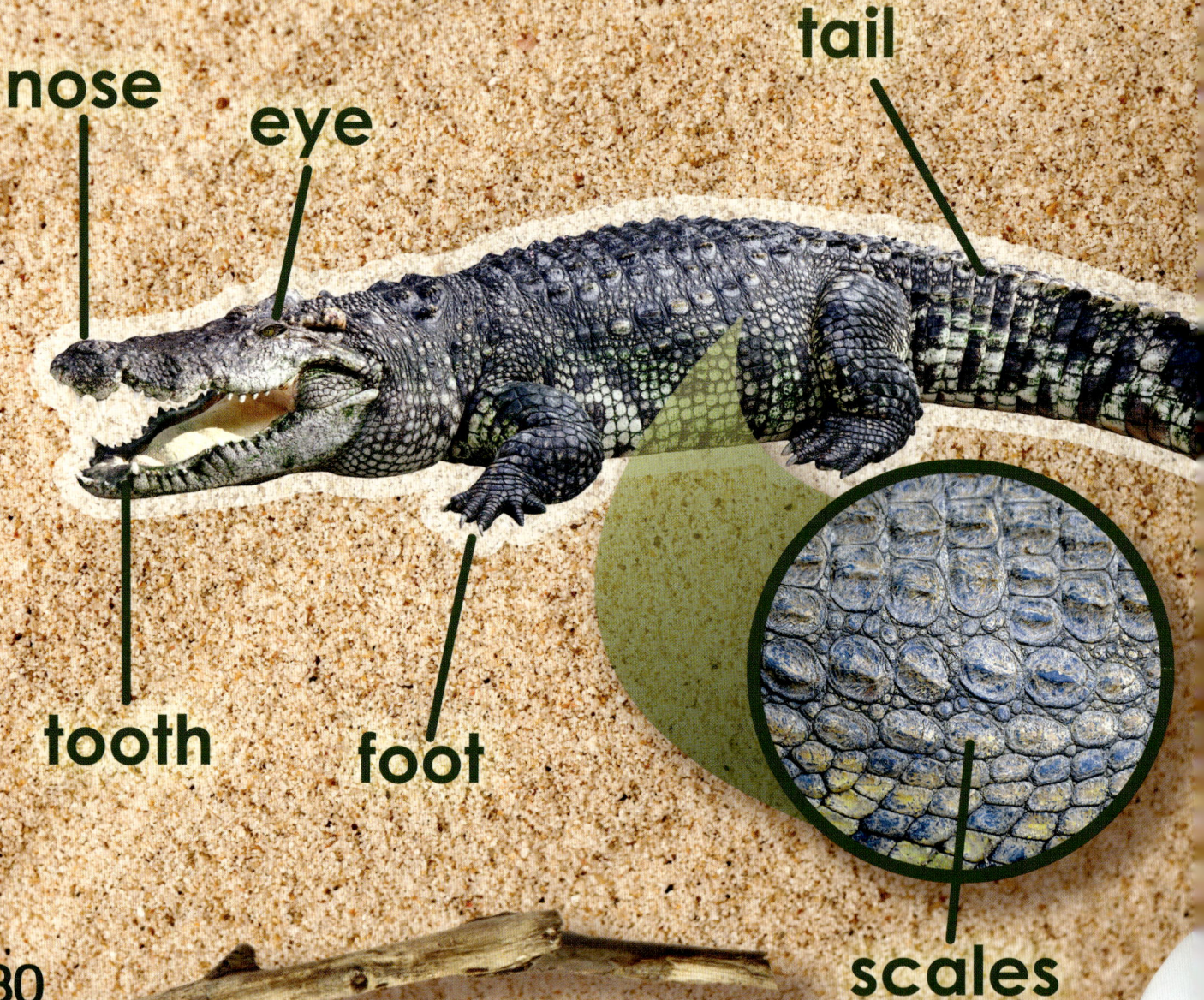

nose

eye

tail

tooth

foot

scales

I can use the first letter sound to match the word to the picture.

tooth

lizard

nest

crocodile

POWER WORDS
How many can you read?

a	come	in	on	up
am	do	is	one	want
an	get	it	that	what
and	go	live	the	where
are	have	lots	there	why
big	he	me	they	will
can	here	my	this	with
can't	I	of	to